The Real Ethereal

Katie Naughton

The Real Ethereal
© 2024 Katie Naughton

Design and layout by Brad Vogler

Cover photo by Annie Spratt

ISBN: 978-0-9991037-9-1
Library of Congress Control Number: 2024938446

Delete Press
deletepress.org

Contents

the world   lets   you leave
it wide   live   that wild
rasp   that
reed that wind
that weed
rooted

making and
unmaking

poems before
poems for
poems after

day book

day book

waking up I can smell time behind my head a paraffin burning
                              gentle as morning as the coffee brewing
in the kitchen the timer I set
last night and poured the water and grounds I try to make
                              choices about what choices to make

winter finding me unwilling slicing fruit stored in summer
                              into ever smaller disks
I dream I steal a job
from my brother my mind goes fallow the dark ridges
                              want the frost the sun to sink
the red light to drain
stick wet leaves to the shoes coming in the door alone
                              the chill of illness the sliding
sounds of daily being
making patterns therefore meaning this job takes me time
                              I take this job and need it
mean it into sound
sounding sure being sick washing dishes making coffee
                              stack stack
the days the border I make from labor take what is not
mine from mine

the billowing bright day is gone we did not
                    have the money to keep it
the picture taken
upstairs the light and heat coming through
                    the window then the house
torn down the waste mass
of drywall plaster and beams that was the most
                    money I ever knew and so much
is not enough and more
is destructive the image world surrounds us is what
                    someone could buy or buy next to
even the ocean is someone
else's now I sort my waste carefully return materials
                    to earth and industry and cities
pull themselves down over
and over return themselves to fire return themselves to ocean
                    a new continent gyres we cannot
find someone willing
to buy our garbage the ritual the smallest pieces let them
                    enter into your blood
make you plastic like an ocean

every two hours and forty-
one minutes someone puts the last armful of items into
                              the car and drives
one of the roads spiraling out
east or south of the warehouse-lined roads out of town
                              and does not come back
headed west southwest
like one early December early evening one hundred
                              geese shout through the sky

the light that's thrown against the window
presses outside into
                    the street or where
my neighbors walking by can see it
proof of each
                    other this long
year two strings in sparkling drape
almost pastel
                    colored copper star
candelabra arc like the windows I'm told
in Stockholm
                    the lights inside
a city window a proximity a life
I did not live
                    but saw or
entered as a relative or guest the difference
momentary between
                    occupant and occupy

the image world shimmers in our neighbor's windows
the vacant house

                  and who left it
pink hearts and red a sugar crystal glitter
in winter

               in lights
the image of my body thick and sound
a mitten

               in me
for holding a hand or more mettle
pushes through

               me
hysterical and serious calm lying on the floor
my body

               near my self
receding into momentary plainness
of blood

               some thing
simple and wrapped in a thick red blanket
with you

               and everything
everything that's alright when something's
really

               wrong

hour song

my love in strange places

morning takes me take the street traffics
daily time through me though morning
comes already strange and I leave
the choirs of history and their small bells
strange for the mornings I woke not home
and so made everything new measured time
walked to breakfast the street waking unknown
a song takes me back 80s hits MJ
Stevie Nicks falling over and over
morning love and losing it heaven
on earth is the bored morning my love
in strange places in strangeness of sleep
a song asks me again take your body
take you home someplace we've never been before

you home some place we've never been before
winter sidewalks the city sky traffics
up the avenue the river lighted
red even in one time winter I make
you the city a bowl of red waiting
the edges I wait you wait the weather
we were here once stood under the neon
late light and cold you were eating bread
you were someone else I took you and you
again to one corner second and ninth
changes day fares people passed while time while
most things stay mostly things you again you
eating me making you home again red
weathered time my love returns a city

the chorus of history stopped the snow falls
all afternoon I stay inside my loves
industry I keep me under snow warm
in sleep the snow stops the house the light
comes down my love in darkness unmakes me
making time dinner the lamp of kitchen
window throws against the eves you don't
fit in this poem your silences your distance
your time your kitchen you in my kitchen
in my silent time you making you me
of sleep and failing light the wrong turn
that history kept on while I did not
saying to me my my my time you you
do exist you do exist you do you

o that heat

time our oldest song the wind wilt blow
unwell across the plains the speed
in gathered distance I wish there were
a poem of every place and every one I've been
and when and who with me and what I did
not see then people end the earth turns o-
ver what meaning there to not re-
member never see   too late
some days to even ask people lost
to speech a mind a cactus
a small bright room some people
you cannot call to some people are what you have
done earth turns over round the sun
earth turns over earth turns o that heat

warms to it and itself wants it finished
you don't finish you return again morning
against sleep the body house in case
of mind of bone was a place you stayed time
be cause brain be matter give birth your
mother cannot stay yet she holds
your baby her body your mother her
dying and one afternoon not finished
snowing one couch you all there not waiting
or   she has her feet in mountains
she made lead of her body up the peaks
this is how the stone glints hot sun shines while
the sky takes its wind from the ocean
trees dark as shade shade her cool the time

day afternoon letters the scraps of you
remain I saved some words yours your hands
pressure here far away when what I
have is nothing worth saying said
I am learning   to stay still
to save the time to still in sweat heat
the afternoon to wait the sun out no
money enough for that worth of time
dying comes quiet sends no postcards
        you always remember to write
from within the silent house when you wait
for night to come will come a day will come
to my regret how the time weights in on
the house that kept its tidy morning to

is what I take you for the sunflower hill
in Nebraska a man stops his pickup
like it is god's country on his face the yellow high
of all those flowers to tell me about it
the rain was different this year this year
we made a lake where our faces should have been
the vacation and the ease of motor oil my heart
should be sage on the dry edge of dying
my god's country that sweet in the sun
of change the worn metal inevitability
these hills traded on the streets of Omaha
and string the wire pave the road the disaster
comes in sunflowers and purple aster
every Sunday mundane as the day breaks

your minutes in Augusts

how big my god the lonely world
holds us in hollows of its
blue dying eyes my grandfather
came back downstairs to talk
about the Wisconsin dells vacations
their geography how the word
lived past its meaning its afternoon
its last time saying the man
a place I had never been with him
a place I stopped for gas going back
to Minnesota one horizon
the rock and sky trees moving in wind
shaded water in a place with no sound
asphalt road and green and grass and grass

failed to attend you haze on the horizon
        storm coming in sudden
windy   dinner cooling on the air
promising water promising plains I never
was childhoods bicycling fifty years
before I was in the rain on my birthday
the cake inside my family inside
waiting held there in time waiting backwards
to their birthdays their bicycles parents
in the dress of the day butter yellow
seersucker bright madras French dots
milk glass beaded porcelain butter cream
some days those days we left our families
left the house ourselves to rain and pine

time our oldest song

to make an expanse one who lies
in the oaken sun to make a circle under
the trees the past we made ourselves look like
the dinner like families like mine on a farm
small time oat grower in Minnesota
before a city life you return
archetype when I sleep your woman
body lake water silted red up
the dry creek a bed a dark room you far
from me and in the same room you turn from
me in sleep I have not attended you
slipping blossoms out every part that swells
turgid were born this season will die
the drought the flood I miss again and may

to make plain an expanse to lay oak
as floor to face attention a sanctity
heat to scent in the air cold body
water makes us under enduring sun
summer comes in from the cold tide
time our oldest song the wind wilt blow
blossom out the boughs as a flute for
-sythia you had a body you have it
still when I miss you your body
in Michigan was mine in New Haven
first on Easter I was twenty-four
I had left New York to stay all night
with you the morning was cool had rained
the riot of green when I drove away

warming ending what it may you persist

dawn is not mine day still breaks yellow
outline the windowsill springs my room
my preparations the things your postcard thaws
careful failing provisions the worn song
the country morning whether it runs cold
the river swelled the fat April drops   ·
express of clouds to ground already over
-turned ready earth in wide ribs
I wait warm season for you
some morning through that screen bright
air in time I try to end to trail my fingers
(the frozen pond the geese announce but where
are you   )

the loss you cannot lose it dogs you come
up the hill at day's pond the car blue
as sky as water we swim one side one side
pleating in the water laps the hair floats
one family has two sides one afternoon
with one aunt one second cousin who dies
out her breath my grandmother who loses
first some vision then some speech then cannot
move but not yet today the family a body
the water a closed ring closed hour around
our sound the day a closed bright thing here
inside it your thoughts blaze here inside
later a hospital room drawn as broken breath
our gone already carried in our mouths

what to make of it but run late at night
when all the heat is earthed the sun
the other side of the world past dark fields
widest skies and night vision the red low
barn holed through with weather my body then
my body and yours night in the field there
of growing trees where I left me against you
in the wind through the summer leaves in the dark
how I leave in my sneakers leaving home
running after a family a teenage feeling
I left was left became older
I became you became family and you
in a house in a field lit at night
left a remainder of me

was time what gathered you in and time what
sends you back out the summer returned
in green in fields in insects when we walk
evenings after eating after heat
and snow on peaks past the plain we didn't make
it far enough did not leave our time like wind
when we leave across the plains again late
evening the traffic still around the town
the gas stations and what else they sell late
the fast food chains the light changes we leave
the night behind a Bruce Springsteen song
we cannot bear to sit around a fire
with each other and sing we drive each other
up the closest hill we say what kills us

up the brown hill

runs off the backs of what we have not burned
time again turns returns the small
parade small town I left you came back
broker and with a richer accent to sit
again in the house where time passes
like in dreams suspended and waiting
like there's not the whole world out there wasn't
there slow afternoons early slip of night
slow time on the floor this is the place I wasn't
alone in memory the town pulled down trees
tore down the park built close houses we lived
in small woods like the whole world wasn't
in snow in summer waiting for us to go

in small woods like the whole world wasn't
we were trying to catch fish and didn't
and wanted to eat them carry them up
the hill on bicycles too hard to pedal
should have known was an easy place to fall
from to edge around the small valley child
-hood made of the place your father at night
in his cold swimming pool you still fish your
father died I wrote you my first poem you
and my brother you stayed he left came
back the valley you canoe the Matta-
besset past the sewage there are meadows
Connecticut you drink too much you grow
your beard you do not rest the swimming pool
untended you fill it with what you catch

runs off the backs of what we have not burned
Connecticut river through brown stone brought
to Brooklyn the elevated body
another river abstracted valley
the money made work made the 1840s
a hole in the ground fills with rain
and rust the time does into us
in the morning I become no one leave
your bed before dawn up the river drive
home (Portland: come on over) to work break-
fast make the coffee for the world to make
the world to make the small return
of time the day came up today again
up the brown hill the other side I see it

up the brown hill the other side I see it
quiet lay the hills lay on the hills light
afternoons snow books birches the college
made of library windows sheets of light
lay on the hills snow before the dark comes
down the valley the other side the water
made mills made canals made Utica
third city millions then rust how valley
fell into light and time into water goes
back to Manhattan I didn't know I
was reading money's war reading Em-
erson the richest I was and was not
in the library to try to see the hill
and valley before the dark comes down

the question of address

the question of address

I know you were there
in the time I passed
through spent
in places and time you
coming near me passing
away. I know we spoke
worked alone or together
in a room or outside
while the day while year.
I may have written you
or spoken
more silently in time.
What was your voice?
Was mine? I remember
some of you and some of you
I don't but mostly I
don't write or speak
to you anymore.
I write these poems.
I put you in here.
The places we were
are still as vigil. I open
a window slight hear
the traffic come inside.

the question of address (poem for a scientist)

you the ideal   for what I want
to tell *you, you*
receiving   beyond reception.
I make myself
present   to *you*
          (trying to keep thinking)

Sometimes *you're*   someone. Some times
're someone   else   Some times
some things surround   .

(The kitchen, where I fell in love with you in love with a widower
and his three-year-old son and making me acorn squash with sheep's
milk manchego and some other fall vegetables, how I went home to
New York and knew on the north side of Houston walking west past
a small garden on a wet day with a former lover that I was waiting for
you, which I did, happily through the winter, though it may not have
looked anything like waiting to me or anyone else.)

This letter misplaced   is wrongly dispatched
          (thinking is self ish   takes me a long   time)

the question of address (poem for a scientist)

Nietzsche saying all philosophy is autobiography, by error.

Or Keats the reverse: "Axioms in philosophy are not axioms until they are proved upon our pulses."

And science tries to erase you from it   but cannot;

(Your life in it, your hours at the lab, your slow laptop borrowed from your mother from her psychology department running and crashing the hours of analysis, the method you used nearly obsolete by the time you finished the writing, shows the history of your funding, your advisor's relationship with you and with his department, your perfectionism. The time spent cooking, making wedding cakes, spent on the shady shore of a small lake with me on Sundays, spent taking pictures of birds in a nest, spent in and out of trains and cars and airplanes to see me, your mother, your brother and his daughter. Everything you felt obscured in science's passive voice. Science obscured it. You obscured it. But the work is yours. Your work to make it yours.)

(I am in it, too, how I hated it, waiting for you at the window of your lab at dusk, throwing sticks at the window lit with you measuring reagents and mixing media for your yeast cultures to grow in, your unwieldy anxiety about starting and finishing, how we could not go anywhere because of it, how you were never done; but also loved it, being let in, the big oak door, Yale's old stone castle of an environmental biology building, to your brilliance, the warmth and light in the messy piles of papers and stacks of jars of coffee growing mold, waiting for you there, and all it gave me access to, in my wool sweaters and leather shoes, my tidy intelligent face and well-kept hair, passing unnoticed into the libraries of the academy their dark and bright wood.)

(I am there but no one would recognize me, nor am I the subject of your work or object of it. Here *you* are.)

If you were here, I would have   told you   everything I could say
a gift and   what I extracted

lost, little bright fragments   propositions
something like   texture
a life with   without you
addressed in terror

What else could I have written? :

the question of address (transmission)

I become nothing in my waiting
into time
like it is one afternoon in Ithaca,
New York, I remember you but I
can't see your faces you were
a fabric a field
in which I moved buoyed
by the water in a pool
in a gorge in bright summer

Time as home
in time as a trace
I survived myself
was what I subtracted from myself
was what was left

I wait on the edges
the time of my body
my body of time:
gathers
tides

But *I* but *you* like two antennas the whole plains
spread between us vibrating great and still
brown bright grasses their sound the wind
at night the whole sky the ocean the other side
of what we never leave
the whole dark expanse and all the bodies
you and all the light it contains

the question of address (poem for a scientist)

from silence we
go into silence

the work of night
time the emptied

thought's form
how you fit it

to your self
to what rigor

asks takes

I miss
you listen I

let
you loosen

what I
made you

know

proof:

let there
be

what I do
not know

when I
do not know

you

one kind of waiting
is for something finished
to become unfinished

one kind of waiting
is to know what you
do not want to know

one kind of silence
is lying one kind
of lying is waiting

one kind of knowing
is not possible
one kind of telling

is what I tried
I waited one time

there were a lot of poems
I wrote for you
that you could see
the rooms and bridges
bodies of water
of our lives
together

your poems were something
other
or depending on how
I mean poems
your poems
were the same

the question of address (elegy: apartment)

with you I have reached
the limits of reason with you
described the trajectory
you had two chairs and mine
was never close enough
at breakfast I want to you
close to you be to you
I tell you everything I see
the kitchen every day I map
my heart the morning for you
the cat circles us lies in the sun
the large room at the top
of the old house
everything I said to you failed
it my self and the limits
of what I could know I felt

moving day (elegy: earth)

The interruption of thought into feeling
to speak about it without project, proposition
Is what I take you for
to find you on the sunflower hill

nothing like what I lose
how I am emptied out in the interstices
alone in my room asleep
the afternoon like it is god's country
how I seek

The violence in it, spike and shoot and goldenrod
is it the violence of love, religion, industry
daily desire, for work, for some new thing,
for the night, for someone else
to make dinner, clean the dishes
we make blue
what we take and keep

Not statistics the anecdote *the rain was different this year*
this year it was
we are more certain of the warming earth than of the vacation
our American vacation and the ease of motor oil

is a disease of the body this failure of sight, heart
my mother's world for seven generations, ruined nerve
the world continues though
when what we are after leaves us for dead

Against the telephone in my car
I drive across the country
of you in your life and me in mine
I pause before descending

spend a night in the Nebraska hills
pitch a tent alone
in the wind watch a storm come on over a Western lake
in the high plains filling in a canyon behind a dam
listen to the generators switch off at 9pm
when the people in the RVs parked by the shore turned off their lights
and go to sleep bleary with the altitude the miles

I traded my one life for another
when I drove on the broadly spread streets of Omaha
I drove away from you

and the damage we made
each of us slowly making our money
would be paid on by each person of the rest of the world
would show itself in the rice on another continent
in the exports in the next century
in the fortunes told
in the absence of religion
in subsidized wheat in Nebraska

for the run from reason
for the failed economies of ecology and oil
for what we called free
we took and waved at the feet of our mother
but did not lay it down in prayer

the question of address (elegy: mill city)

orange clawfoot tub
bathroom sink in the kitchen
dentures in a plastic deli tub

linoleum
fifty-year-old gas stove faulty pilot
percolator coffee
toast crumbs
Polar diet soda orange dry
window full of cactuses
refrigerator magnets the American Southwest Alaska
Catholic holy places

rounded edge of green beer refrigerator
galley kitchen tight and dark
He's trying to tell eighty-year-old women how to wash dishes
the glasses I took the pots and pans
once no one lived there before the stuff was gone
the washing machine and dryer
took three old cousins to take it out
a few steps down the cellar stairs
back up the stairs and out the kitchen door

the dirt floor basement
stacks of sheet metal and the tools to work it
Cut once measure twice
burnt out old apartment towards the back
had linoleum had windows had a family of cousins living in it
before they moved upstairs
wet burnt dirt and oil smell

Ballentine green can
bright sharp yellow smell
cigar smoke
it's naptime

hating naptime
Kelly green suit for Sundays and holidays
old leather chair hard red leather
I take a birthday cake towards it
you don't have to if you don't want to
Ballentine green cans made into a prop plane hung above it
brass bent into model tall ships on the table next to it
how to never move all day

shelves and lost shelves of frog figurines
big jars of hard candies all taste like mint like fruit
I aspirate one once lay on the couch
with the knot of it against my spine until it is gone
the pictures of the cousins the grandkids
the big eighties high school hair
a white ceramic cat a candle never burned smells like wax roses

one room in the back I never go in
one room in the back the old things are in
dungarees swimsuits sweatshirts from Cape Cod

above-ground pool round and cold
sharp and bad smelling grass the roaming dogs of the neighborhood
the city dirt
the sidewalkless road the crumbling asphalt
the hedges torn through by a small tornado
the bird bath out front the porch the stairs to the second floor
the cousins the motorcycle on the front sidewalk the hot vinyl seats
the poison ivy in the lattice shiny and green

the bedroom a dark place dark wood
and worn down dark red woven mat on the floor
when I sleep here I sleep in the bed too
spiral curl of carved wooden banisters
spots in the tiles of the ceiling
I watch TV from bed eat a piece of gum all the way through

do you want to go to 7-Eleven now? // Is it time yet?
I get sick when we are downtown lie in the bed
while the people are talking in the house
the dresser where the things are lipstick the jewelry I am given
the blue glass votive light the Virgin
the mid-century photos
Peggy Ann
in nurse's whites
John Joseph
an army mechanic
your father
with a radical's facial hair
when it's night the streetlight through the windows
the porch is there
the front door opens to the stairs the dark indoor stairs
to the cousins upstairs
Aunt Jo's, David Dodge.
there is not really a front door to downstairs
the entryway opens to the bedroom
we come in through the front the bedroom or we come in
through the back the kitchen
there's a key under the mat in the back

the question of address (elegy: suburbs)

some questions never leave the garage the basement
the hedges and other plants circling the house
the rock wall stratifying the small hill in the back yard
between oaks and wax begonias
a house can be a place you never leave
it can be the hatch door to the basement
the bare construction of stairs
a place to carry a bicycle up or down
a machine no more beautiful than complex
the asphalt path outside domestic enough
a thin layer slowly shaped by roots as dirt would be
as the oaks grow summers come and go
tracking back and forth that route between basement
garage past plantings past a screened porch
a neat lifetime of things the cared-for cars
every license plate marking state and time
lost aesthetics of childhoods grown quite old
the small secret half-room a ledge under the stairs
still possible to climb into a house within a house
a room within a room stooped ceiling short table
the time passed there half-outside half-inside a family

the real ethereal

the hearing of moths

what she leaves behind
where she did not go
who she was not

                                         she said I could stay
anytime her last house
the bed moved out

the money of a lifetime was how they stayed here
got here

                                         one person whose life
came at the rate it came
paid at the rate that was
how far can you get
in one lifetime how long do you
wait to go home how
do you have

                                         how to keep going
because you have to
everything taken
everything given

                        mean
                        ordinary
                        time

the big room will be taken
on   by
someone else

this wood this light
this glass and metal world

                                          will call it home
                                          held

the ecstatic

                                          maddening
                                          crash
                                          through time

bathing costumes
percolators
meatless Fridays
refrigerator magnets

                                          the phone rang
                                          the tub rusted

the dream

                                          rented
                                          and dreamed

time pulling
wet
heavy
at her heels

look at the trees their August shade
from the window of your life your one window
from the bedroom from the stairs
you went up and won't come down again
the heat, the house, the laundry and breath
done there
your minutes transit the house from the bed
of all Augusts
same silent heat wind sun shade still
of time gathered there, that room
I lay on the floor
your child and not
the blonde wood and white linen
soap and ceiling
you had a room once
a bicycle a dusty road
the oak shade the sun
in another state
as children do
as I did
do
switch me out
one August hour
one August
for ours
for another

holy science

the most of the most porous
the hearing of moths

that you walk out your door
all is there is road

                all generous
                even

the shadows lay thick across
your hand like weight like water

passed through a bright ring

sleep, morning
you

what birthed summer
me

my twenty-eight years
in pieces

(not my letters not my minutes not   my hand)

the city doesn't come off us
not in waves like heat diffusing
in the irregular air around us

                              me I know
                              money
                              second-hand

dressed lunchtimes
a shining wall

                         always heard
                         caught smooth
                         in the throat

the sounds themselves
partake of light
through deep water
sun the deeper
water the nearer
the glass world
built of air

                         in melting ice
                         the lemonade
                         in the weft of thick
                         cotton

summer money's
season

the daylight will
the weather of the water

the air turns
hot

         poor
         careful

dust
blooms

           and what is mine?
           some things I came by
           take some space

full and blank
people
drawn from
circumstance
by
sun

this is the moment
of crisis
this
is the crisis

money
could be had
by making
it
in a city
of one kind
handmade
money
I
join
some world   its
seamed promise
(not ?)
at odds
  the woods
  the edge of
  suburban
  sub-
  developments
some houses
  banks
rivers and buildings
equals
not
equivalent
I
make
work

what I took
was mine
was the city

        what I took
        was mine
        was unready

I take
your silence

why record
any thing

        poems after
               after
               after
               after

instead of eternity returned
the email the front door
a glyph of the subdivision
the river a place nobody goes
lined with small garbage
flat brown pebbles
where someone imagined safety
like rain will miss us when
we go we go

who will keep my body?
dust? ordinance?

the shadows tracking
the edge of the lake?

rot
membrane of
                the safety we bought
                the whorl of a fingerprint
                a telephone

        frayed nerve
        the pools of the heart

when the day turns over
        day turning over to night
interstices and years
        what you give is
what you take away
        o worse
o better nothing

the morning
brings the frost
when what you have done
        is the sunflowers
and other weeds

        is time and
season
and you
        have a body
and so do I

        is what I
take
you for

the water boils
the evening spins

a second singing

the city

                resists my room
                my small brown room

a chestnut half buried in mud
a hard brown shell in spring

                an Easter

where do I put myself and why?

on Sunday now I stay in bed –
                rest

the morning as though –

these formal histories

remain?
and October?

of the light and water
stone   rain   the city

some part of what I'll say
is obscured
in these materials

call them what I won't return to
call them what is lost what was left
when I spend an afternoon
restless and looking

what do I think
it is
I am trying to tell you

winter coming
stepping in the door
looking back to shut it
that grey bright sliver of street
that change of someone passing

Some days are my inheritance
gray and November I want
to see out of them and also
to be inside them though
the endless dissipation the body
turning to heat to waste pass
or spend a life its imagined
or remembered textures. So most time
stopped to remember happens
in an empty room with the internet
the flat word of the screen
standing in for some other place
where something happens. The
news is who stays poor in
the necessary rooms waiting
for dinner. I'm in some threshold
looking through two doors.
The rooms are empty but feel
like weight   like world.

how many more days can begin with dim light
the half-asked question the glimpse the window
of winter wouldn't these songs weather it
the time it takes to make a living the past
isn't even an elegy I find
the family name in the white pages
of the city the heavy phonebook paper
and ink my eyes want to leave my body sell
me some scent something to brighten my mouth
I want a building to wait in means the part
that's missing means means enough
to live on /lencten/ means before
history we saw the light coming back

stay home alone the weekend make time
ecstatic spool not everything's elegy
even dying seconds being alone
thinking back alone at night and young new
york late moving the body the city
living the light and space between the fine
edge of   feeling the other
sidewalk or platform above or below
or next to the traffic what enigma
of history I mean walking mean I want
to feel the feeling again almost un-
safe having so little and so much
time and now and now and now and now and

the generous
      moment
       so full of plants
sound of insects
         passing cars sometimes
static forms
   buildings
   sky
I
want
   more
than anything
        evaporating
        on the sidewalk
August
        after the rain
some time
       so distant
       it's dying
is too
what I
       'll hold
      out

easy listening

movement of locust leaves movement
of air moving the leaves a breath a flight
fluid above it quick hinge of wing gliding
starling before the stars the late light
of May time a breath a movement
the air around the legs mine I will
place myself here in this time
of hazed bluing gold light a sound
a movement the muscle my leg makes
a strength out and out across
the street in front of the house this evening

*

I'm telling you the color of the light in the hills
at the end of the day when it is warm
has rained I'm saying the words wax begonia

*

all night on the edge of sound
everyone else is inside of

*

it's six hundred dollars
to fly across an ocean
I'm waiting
something changes & I don't know it

*

it's the detail of when the sun is setting
it's the lilac white and purple
it's the red of the small house
the vertical boards the rise
of their ribs from the surface

*

in bed the world contracts
to your exhausted eye
opening
a last time
for me
lasting
again and again
named a last time
into what
I don't know

*

things being what they are

*

a coin is the state made flat and concrete
listening at the window
gold and shining
the hours of the buildings
the small lamps in the windows
the pushcarts of newspapers
children and their parents

*

I could believe in what is real
as the reflective surface
cutting the kitchen in half
reaching into its milky replication
the sink the oven a family
is as simple as this a child
a window opened again
as simple as this a family

*

as though the sun's daily metaphor
across the sky were not ecstatic transport
return return return return return
it's only ever always space and time

*

throwing my shoulder forward
recognition of the jaw held fast
in the mouth in the middle of the night
sound before phoneme before meaning
body of voice thrown into sound
by what breath   age's gravel
the only mark of unendingness we have
the refusal to stop until stopped

*

peony geranium a terrace &
the water voices coming across
exhaustion's baffle and mostly
otherwise silence I'm told
there's some feeling doesn't need
to be fixed – hours on the shore
diesel boat engine roars
louder than the ear

*

the sun tonight setting after
eleven as far north as we'll go
a few weeks until midsomar
we'll be married we'll save flowers
we'll give what we're given to
everyone the sun spreads
into a crown a flaring
a made place at the edge
of the water and sky

that wild weed

what is the equivalent of tracing out a line in blue water?
I cross the street of a quiet mountain town
where there used to be a railroad
someone who loves me following me
or I am alone looking up at the cool sky
something worn and buzzing around my head

there's a width to the flame of the candle burning
from the size of the wick and the heat of the wax
specific to the material

the book is long or should I say time has passed
I have passed over some threshold I stand
in the same doorway wary the method
nearly obsolete by the time I finished the writing

like a bride or two like coming finally home
like a ring a day a lifetime

like a regular feeling
intensified like a deep
spreading liquid stain
like there's another dark
I hadn't even known
and some calm in having
placed it

it's hard to say I'm here until I'm exhausted
then it's enough to say
the indifference of the sky this rock my own body
is enough hearing water lying in the bed the rain
the things that stay until they don't
good as good is

threshold

like a bride or groom
like finally coming home
an oscillating pair
the weighted center
stretching extending
through the city
down the lakeshore
through the vineyards
in October the end
of the heat in the grape-
globed air in April
the cold of the groundsnow
coming off in waves
in the sun coming out
of the floorboards
a scent of pine and wax
a temperature
a structure of time
we made are making

Notes

26 "and may" is Gertrude Stein.
27 "riot of green" is Adrienne Rich.
30 "teenage feeling" is Neko Case.
49 "moving day (elegy: earth)" is an artifact of a procedure duplicated from Karla Kelsey's *Iteration Nets*.
74 "and now" is Gertrude Stein.

Acknowledgements

A chapbook from the manuscript, *a second singing*, was published by Dancing Girl Press in 2023.

Earlier versions of poems from the manuscript were published in the following journals:

"Drugi śpiew (fragment)," (from "the hearing of moths"), Polish translation by Adam Zdrowski, in *Wizje*.
"moje kochanie w dziwnych miejscach.," ("my love in strange places"), Polish translation by Marta Kolbuszweska, in *Queer Erotica Zine: Girls and Queers to the Front*.
"the question of address," "the question of address (elegy 3: suburbs)"; "the question of address (elegy 4: mill city)," "the question of address (poem for a scientist I)"; "the question of address (poem for a scientist II) in *Interim*.
"Warming Ending What It May You Persist" (1, 3), and from "The Hearing of Moths" in *Snail Trail*.
"Moving Day (Place Elegy 2: Earth)" in *Sixth Finch*.
"day book" [II, III] in *Michigan Quarterly Review*.
"Up the Brown Hill" in *Opon*.
"Warming Ending What It May You Persist (4)" in *Grama*.
"Warming Ending What It May You Persist (2)" on Poets.org.
"Time Our Oldest Song" (as "The Question of Address") in *Flag and Void*.
"My Love in Strange Places (2, 3)" in *Jubilat*.

Thanks

Many thanks to the colleagues, teachers, friends, and family who supported me and this work as it was being made, among them: Melissa Hohl, Abby Chabitnoy, Cedar Brant, Cass Eddington, Gracie McCarroll, Drew Webster, CL Young, Sasha Steensen, Dan Beachy-Quick, Matthew Cooperman, Camille Dungy, Allyson Paty, Ariana Nash, Brent Cox, George Life, Travis Sharp, Myung Mi Kim, Judith Goldman.

For funding and support, thanks to Colorado State University, the State University of New York at Buffalo, the Gray and McNulty Chairs of the Buffalo English department, and Vermont Studio Center.

Thanks to Brad Vogler and Delete Press for the vision and labor that make a manuscript into a book of poems. Thanks to Michelle Turner for copyediting.

And thanks to the editors who published earlier forms of poems from these manuscripts in their journals, and Kristy Bowen at Dancing Girl Press for making a selection of work in this manuscript into a chapbook in 2023.

Most of all Neil FitzPatrick for keeping me keep the faith, and for dinner.

Katie Naughton is a poet living in Brooklyn, NY. She is the author of the chapbooks *Study* (above/ground press, 2021), *A Second Singing* (Dancing Girl Press, 2023), and *Debt Ritual* (forthcoming from Bunny/Fonograf Editions, 2024). Her poetry has been published or is forthcoming in *Fence*, *Bennington Review*, *Michigan Quarterly Review*, *Tupelo Quarterly*, and elsewhere. She holds an MFA in creative writing from Colorado State University and is a doctoral candidate in the Poetics program at State University of New York at Buffalo. She is an editor at Essay Press, the HOW(ever) and How2 Digital Archive Project, and *Etcetera*, an online journal of poetry and poetics.